40 Days & Nights of Passionate Devotions

Saturate yourself in the love of God!

AARON BEACH

Special Thanks

These are the most blessed people on earth! they each contributed heavily to this devotional.

Aunt Bonnie: Over the course of the writing of this book, I learned many things from her. She was instrumental in helping me make sense of God's purpose for this devotional.

Pamela Lynn: She was so supportive and helpful to the utmost. She was the first to read it over and gave suggestions and recommendations right away. She got me excited about the potential of this devotional.

Paula Campbell: Her exhortations and encouragements were much appreciated. She helped me see how powerful the revelation of God's love for us truly is, and how much people need it today.

Pastor Jay Randolph: His wise advice and expert editing contributed to the excellence of the writing. His input and motivating speak helped me soldier through the process of completing the work laid out for me.

Biography & Intro

BY AUNT BONNIE

Aaron Beach was called forward from his mother's womb to become a vessel of honor prepared for God's glory!

My sister, Joddi Beach, received a prophetic word after several daughters and several miscarriages, that she would become a mother of sons (plural). God makes a way for His Word to come to pass when it seems like there is no way through. Obstacles are diminished and, like a flood, God's Holy Spirit lifts up a standard against any enemy and Aaron remains standing!

During her pregnancy, I felt led by the Spirit to send her special vitamins and minerals to prepare her and the baby. So, it was of no surprise when she delivered a healthy male child! Despite the need for an emergency C-section, Joddi healed miraculously quickly! She had no pain, no scar, and was then able to have her 2nd son naturally with no complications at 45-years of age!

Joddi told me of conversations she had with Aaron when he was a young child. He actually was speaking some words at three-months when I first saw him. She said he told her, during early childhood, things about angels and Heaven that he could remember. These could have been from before birth or experienced by visitation in their home, while she composed praise music on keyboard, sang to the Lord, and worshiped for hours upon hours each day!

Aaron was brought up in a Christian home in Warsaw, Indiana. His family attended a spirit-filled congregation. Aaron wasn't always a lover of God. He doubted His existence and pretended to be a Christian all of his childhood. A way was provided for him, while in the 5th grade, to attend a youth conference called, "Acquire the Fire." The Newsboys group was performing and Aaron calls the atmosphere that was expressed spiritually as, "ridiculous love." The atmosphere of Heaven's overwhelming love for Aaron and the desire to accept Jesus as Savior and Lord: manifested! He was convicted to surrender all his heart to Jesus and received the Lord's, "indescribable peace," that passes understanding. Aaron acknowledges that immediately he felt like, "a different person." He was delivered from negative attitudes, fearful emotions, and chaotic discord. He immediately desired to study the Bible and started enjoying church services and church fellowships rather than just going along.

When Aaron, his father, mother, and brother Adam were living in Dayton, Kentucky, during his high school years, they began listening to and participating in the Florida Healing Outpouring Revival with my encouragement. He began calling out for more of God's spirit to fill Him while praising and received the baptism of the Holy Spirit. A week later, He began to receive his prayer language while spontaneously praising the Lord. He began to read the Bible quickly and comprehended at an accelerated understanding. In 2008, he was able to ask God questions in his studies and understand some responses the Lord made to him.

Shortly thereafter, He began his college studies at Gateway Community and Technical College in Kentucky. He was quickened in his mind and intellect. The homeschooled, "math whiz," was soon successfully peer-tutoring many other students. Through the power of the Holy Spirit, he was able to propel them to above average understanding. He illuminated the concepts so that they could comprehend and move ahead in their degrees. He was given favor and became the President of their local Phi Theta Kappa National Honor Society chapter. He ran meetings and set agendas amongst many other overseer tasks. He graduated in 2011 with a degree in Server Administration; he continued to tutor students until relocating with the family to Indiana.

He moved with the family to Fishers, Indiana in 2011. They began attending Discovery Church in 2012 where he remains an active member. He has participated with the worship team at different times as a backup singer, assisted with the youth group, visited with seniors during senior home ministry, managed media for Sunday services, maintained their website, and handled their social media presence.

He attended Charis Bible College Indianapolis and participated in praise and worship with his mother; also forming a group called, "The Merry Band," with other Charis students. They have performed in both Charis Indianapolis and Charis Schererville for worship events and graduations. He has been to Guatemala on a 10-day mission trip per Charis' requirements. He brought his guitar and played in the villages and for the children, making music with other students there.

He graduated in 2017 with an Associate's in Ministerial Studies as did his mother. He began taking a more active role in the senior ministry with Charis students as he took time for a third-year at Charis, while he was working in the technology field full-time. He continued senior ministry by helping assist the leaders with their teachings, by volunteering his keyboard and vocal talents, and over time, taught as an alternate teacher. In 2020, he was put in charge of the senior ministry and holds the position to this day.

In May of 2020, the Lord began to urge him to begin Praise Without Ceasing; an online fellowship for like-minded believers to unite praise, worship, and prayers of agreement for the edification of all to trust in the Lord. His ministry is marked by peace, joy, and love manifesting from God's great grace and glory! As Aaron unleashes God's praise during His podcast ministry, the Lord is able through the Holy Spirit, to make new paths in the desert as He waters the dry ground so it will again blossom as a garden to the glory of our God!

In September of 2020, he began a program of Chaplaincy at Crossroads School of Chaplaincy for Clinical Pastoral Education. He compiled this book at the Lord's urging in the Fall of 2020. As part of his Chaplain program, he writes cards and makes calls to those who have lost loved ones to encourage them, and to fulfill his divine mission to uplift the fallen; help the helpless; give joy for mourning; and to set all God's misplaced and displaced captives free into a new life in Jesus!

Foreword

BY AUNT BONNIE

2 The heavens declare the glory of God, and the firmament showeth His handiwork; 3 Day unto day uttereth speech, and night unto night revealeth knowledge; - Psalms 19:2-3 JPS Tanakh 1917

This new format of devotion daily and praise meditations at night, seeks to follow the tradition of Israel. Scriptures were read daily and parents were exhorted to, "Talk about them when they laid down and when they rose up and when they sat at home and when they walked along the way!" As we rise up, we read His Word and it gives us life and quickens us as we walk along the road. After sitting in His presence at first, we now have the courage and the strength to do His will at all times! As we prepare to lie down, we reflect in the night watches and seasons with awestruck wonder! We see the marvelous works in our lives wrought by His hand, and the praise we offer up, plows ahead for the day to come! We send forth continuous praise and anticipate His victory in all our tomorrows to come! As we pray and praise Him without ceasing, we become a seamless garment of His praise! That praise continues working through our lives, and writes His living Word on our hearts, minds, door posts, and gates: forever and forevermore!

40 DAYS & NIGHTS OF PASSIONATE DEVOTIONS

Days 1-10

Walking into the water

Freedom begins to take shape. Your identity is being established in Him. Your life is being transformed. Your beliefs may be challenged. Your theology may be questioned. Keep your eyes on Jesus and let the Holy Spirit teach you and confirm the Word to you. Do not take my word for it: take His Word! You have started the process of saturation. You will grow in your relationship with the Lord. Be prepared, be committed, and seek Him with your whole heart.

> *PS: I've included related scriptures in the back of the book that pertain to each day and night. Feel free to use them to study, meditate, and dive deeper into the Word of God.*

Day 1

Variety is the Spice of Life!

In all your ways acknowledge Him, and He shall direct your paths. - Proverbs: 3:6 NKJV

If you want to find God's will, you can! Having this desire assures you that you are submitting yourself to His leading. We have been taught to think that there is only one way God has prepared for us. I do not believe that to be the case.

I believe there are times when He gives us flexibility to make our own decisions. There are many different paths to God's plan for your life... and all these paths are good! Variety is the spice of life and our God knows this better than we do.

Trust in Him! Do not get so stressed over a decision. Ask God His point-of-view, follow the leading of peace and do not hold back. The works of your hands are blessed. You are blessed (past tense). Whatever you decide to do will be a blessing to those around you. You are equipped for His calling on your life. You will not miss His will!

Night 1

Look

Look up - you'll see the starry night sky.
Look down - you'll see the grains of sand.
Look forward - you'll see the promised land.
Look behind - you'll see God standing by.

Wherever you fix your gaze, you'll be reminded of God's ways.
Whenever you look about, remember His promises and erase your doubt.
His love is baked into creation.
Every tribe and every nation.

Every mountain and every valley.
Every desert and every sea.
Look at the signs He left for you to find.
Open your eyes and convince your mind!

Surely the God who calls stars by name.
Can deliver you from every flame!
Faithfulness is His identity.
He only leads us to victory!

Failure is not an option.
He's already taken all of our sin!

Keep your eyes on things above.
Let your cares fly away like a dove.

Next time you're feeling down.
Hope in God, and take a look around.

Day 2

Life is Attracted to Life

Jesus said to him, "I Am the Way, the Truth, and the Life. No one comes to the Father except through Me." - John 14:6 NKJV

The more life you get: the more life you want. Jesus is the Way, the Truth and the Life. The more you get of His life, the more you desire it. The desire to seek Him becomes an eternal burning flame of passionate love for our Lord. You desire to know Him above anything else. His life is His love. Life is attracted to life. Get more of His life by spending time with Him!

Night 2

Enough

His love is enough
His goodness is enough
He is more than enough

People will let you down
Situations will bog you down
But God will never let you down

Don't find your worth in what others say or do
Don't validate yourself by the opinions of others
Don't compare yourself with those on similar paths

Only God can show you how valued you are
Only His love can give you validation
Only God is enough

Day 3

Receive His Love

We love Him because He first loved us. - 1 John 4:19 NKJV

You cannot give what you do not have. You cannot give love without first accepting it from God. His love is there for you, but if you do not open the gift, you will not get the benefit of it. Believe He has good stored up for you. Believe He has a great plan for you that goes beyond your desires.

Once you receive His love: you can receive anything from Him. He has everything in abundant measure for you. Receive His love, receive His gifts, and then share them with others!

Night 3

Live to Love

Love is our calling
Love is our purpose
Love is our life
We live to love

We are Your voice
We are Your hands
We are Your feet
We live to love

Bringing hope to the broken-hearted
Bringing healing to the wounded
Bringing family to the orphans
We live to love

Pulling down every enemy stronghold
Pulling down every wall of shame
Pulling down every blessing of God
We live to love

Praise to our Redeeming Savior
Honor to the King of Kings
Glory forever to our Almighty God
We live to love

Day 4

East and West

As far as the east is from the west, so far has He removed our transgressions from us. - Psalms 103:12 NKJV

East is so far from the west that they cannot see the other side. We are so far from sin that we no longer react to it. We cannot see its effects from afar. Our ties have been separated. Our nature does not respond to it. It might as well not exist since we cannot see it or respond to it from where we are.

East and west are on the same line. East is going forward; west is going backward. It is all about perspective. East will never touch west and vice versa. In math class, we were taught that a line goes infinitely in both directions. It is the same with sin and righteousness. The distance between them is never shortened: it is infinite. Grace is infinite: the more you learn, the more distance there seems to be between sin and righteousness. Your righteousness in Jesus is so far from sin that you'll never have to think about it again!

Night 4

Finally I'm Free

You heard my cry and rescued me
Shackled and chained I was bound in sin
Now finally I'm free
Yes I truly believe

Redeemed and set apart
Jesus, You are My Righteousness
Blessed and highly favored by Almighty God
Glory, hallelujah to You

All praise to Your holy name
All glory belongs to our God
Set apart and lifted high
We raise our voices and worship

The Redeemer of our souls
Has delivered us from every destruction
Now we are seated in Heavenly places
With Jesus Christ, Lord of Lords

Grace is our bread and Truth is our wine
We shall partake of Your promises
You've said, "Yes!" to us and we say, "Amen!"
Holy Divine Jesus, we thank You

Day 5

Walk In Peace

And having shod your feet with the preparation of the gospel of peace; - Ephesians 6:15 NKJV

You cannot move forward without peace. Peace will protect you. Paths can get rough, but with adequate foot protection you will trek over it. Sand gets hot and surfaces could burn, but with footwear you will not be affected. Glass and all sorts of sharp objects could be scattered in your way, but with shoes you will not be injured.

Only a son would have access to footwear. Servants and slaves did not get them. You are a precious child of God. He's made sure to provide everything you need. Peace is provided in the Gospel.

Walk in peace toward others and do not allow circumstances to rile you up. The moment you let go of your peace, you have chosen to make your journey more difficult. You've taken off your shoes in the midst of the walk! Jesus desires for you to stay in peace because peace protects you and draws others to Christ.

Night 5

Not Alone

You are not alone
You are not forsaken
You are not too far
He's reaching for you
For you are His child
And He wants to hold you
He's always with you
Never will He leave
Your Father watches over you

(Father)
You are My child
I want the best for you
I know what you need
Your desires and dreams
I gave them to you
For a bright future
And a prosperous life
Let Me help guide you
I love you

Day 6

Flow in the Current

For He says: "In an acceptable time I have heard you, And in the day of salvation I have helped you." Behold, now is the accepted time; behold, now is the day of salvation. - 2 Corinthians 6:2 NKJV

Time is a current. It's flowing forward. Jesus is the current. We are flowing in Him.

The blood of Christ is the River of Life. We flow with Him. Things flow now. Healing flows now. Miracles flow now. Provision flows now. Everything we need flows now.

His current moves you forward. Everything you need is available right now! Jesus is not withholding anything from you. He is the same yesterday, today, and forever. He propels you forward into all goodness and blessing. Get with His current! Thank Him for His promises! Drink of the Water of Life; expect to receive now!

Night 6

Waterfall of Love

You pour out Your love
And You keep pouring and pouring
Everything is saturated in
Your waterfall of love
Waterfall of love

It fills me and keeps filling me until I'm overflowing
And I can't contain it and it spills out on all those around
me
Everything is soaked
In Your waterfall of love
Waterfall of love

Your flowing love renews my soul
And restores my strength
My whole being is bathed
In Your waterfall of love
Waterfall of love

We are drenched
We are cleansed
We are refreshed
Under Your waterfall of love
Waterfall of love

Our wells can't contain it all
Our rivers have overrun their banks
Our springs are flooding
We are full of Your waterfall of love
Waterfall of love

Jesus, we choose to stand under
Your flowing crimson fountain
Source of Grace and Truth
The Living Waterfall of Love
Waterfall of Love

It will never run dry
It cannot be contained
It will not subside
Your waterfall of love
Waterfall of love

Your waterfall of love
Waterfall of love

Day 7

Like Your Father

Train up a child in the way he should go, and when he is old he will not depart from it. - Proverbs 22:8 NKJV

Children learn from their parents. They learn how to think, behave, live, love, and interact. Some kids grow up wanting to be like daddy or mommy.

We have a Heavenly Father. We were made in His image. He wants us to think, behave, live, love, and interact like Him! He desires for us to be like Him! That's why He gave us His Word: to instruct us in the paths of righteousness. Take His Word, read it, study it, apply it and you'll become more like Your Father!

Night 7

Someone

I thought that I was alone
I didn't know Someone was with me
All this time
I was lost but You picked me up and carried me on Your
shoulders
And then I knew
When I was struggling...

It was You holding my hand
It's always been You by my side
Never letting me out of Your sight
Even though I didn't know You
You never gave up on me
You overflowed my life with Your love
I couldn't resist anymore
My heart of stone was shattered
You gave me Your own
I just knew that Someone was there
And that Someone
Was You

When I think of all You've brought me through
I can't help but rejoice
For I'm alive because of You
So I pour out my praise

And I bless Your name
For there is none like You
Who loves me like You do

I needed Someone to rescue me
And that Someone
Was You

Day 8

Body Heat

Arise, shine; For your light has come! And the Glory of the LORD is risen upon you. - Isaiah 60:1 NKJV.

Body heat is a constant. Enough people in a room will change the temperature due to their body heat. How much more does the Holy Spirit change the atmosphere? The physical realm is a shadow of the spiritual. His glory radiates from our spirit!

Light brings warmth and comfort. Darkness is the absence of light. It brings comfort to know what you are seeing. Coldness is the absence of heat (warmth). Exhibiting the life of the Holy Spirit will light up a dark or heat up a cold atmosphere. Praise, worship, thanksgiving, Fruit of the Spirit, and Gifts of the Spirit will greatly transform the atmosphere!

Night 8

Flawless

You are flawless
Jesus, You are matchless in every way

No face is more beautiful than Yours
Your eyes burn brighter than the stars
Diamonds pale in comparison to Your skin

Spotless Lamb of God: the Perfect Sacrifice
The Crimson Fountain no words can do You justice
Sparkling, redeeming, precious blood of Christ
Washes everything clean in a glowing white

Kingly majesty and unparalleled splendor surround Your throne
Joy unspeakable and peace unexplainable embrace all in Your presence
Your love warms the cold heart and Your goodness soothes the aching soul
Your kindness blows away the fog of confusion and Your faithfulness breaks through every circumstance
Incomparable Grace guides us into all Truth

What more can we say?
What words could come close to describing the fullness of Your Glory?

Every breath we've ever taken and every word mankind has ever spoken doesn't amount to a single note in the grand symphony of music that is You

Eternity isn't near long enough to satisfy our desire to worship, praise, and thank You

We are forever grateful, eternally thankful, timelessly appreciative, and undoubtedly devoted to You

Flawless Jesus

Day 9

Appreciate God

16 Rejoice always, 17 pray without ceasing, 18 in everything give thanks; for this is the will of God in Christ Jesus for you. - 1 Thessalonians 5:16-18 NKJV

When something appreciates: it grows in value. When you appreciate God for all His goodness towards you: He becomes more valuable to you! You will trust Him more. You will believe His Word more strongly. You will hear His voice more clearly. You will receive from Him easier. It all flows from appreciation or in other words... thanksgiving.

Give thanks to Jesus for healing, prosperity, peace, joy, faithfulness, freedom from sin, His perfect promises, righteousness, love, eternal life, Heaven, favor, blessings, your talents, your gifts, your family, your spouse, your house, your friends, your community, your church, your health, your vehicle, your country, your calling, your purpose, your pets, your future, your food, your water, your electricity, the weather, the beauty of nature... there are no shortage of things we can thank Him for! Appreciate God for all He's done for you!

Night 9

Everything to Me

I saw you take your first breath
I watched you take your first step
You've brought such joy to Me
I'm so glad I created you

As a doting Father
My desire is to bless you
My thoughts are to prosper you
I will always be available to you

Nothing in all the universe
Can ever change My mind about you
Love will always encompass you
I will protect you at all times

You are worth it to Me
And if I had to choose again
I'd choose you every time
You mean everything to Me

Day 10

The Ultimate Program

As His divine power has given to us all things that pertain to life and godliness, through the knowledge of Him who called us by glory and virtue - 2 Peter 1:3 NKJV

Jesus is the Ultimate Program. He works everywhere He's installed into. He has given us all things that relate to life (health, peace, provision, adventure, relationship) and godliness (authority, character, righteousness).

Need healing? Install the Great Physician program into your heart. Need provision? Install the Faithful Father program into your heart. Need comfort? Install the Prince of Peace program into your heart. Whatever promise you need: scripture has an app for it!

- Locate the promise in the App Store (find in the Bible).

- Learn about the app (Read & meditate on the promise).

- Install and use the app as much as you want (Speak it out to apply it).

Night 10

Have and to Hold

I was shattered
You faithfully and carefully put me together
Now I know who I am

I was cracked
You repaired me with steadfast love
Now I can store Your goodness

I was dull
You painted me with Your beautiful grace
Now I'm living in color

I was surrounded by danger
You placed me into Your protected collection
Now I'm safe and secure in Your trust

I'm Your handmade creation
Display me for all to see
I'll stand out amongst the broken pots

You're the Potter
I'm Yours to mold
To have and to hold

Then You'll find another one
Who cries out to You
And You'll begin the healing process anew

Review Days 1-10

Salvation

Receiving a new wineskin: new wine cannot go into an old wineskin

Now, that you have had a taste of Jesus in these first 10 days; what are you thinking?

- Are you being encouraged?

- Do you have a better understanding of God?

- Do you believe your relationship with the Lord has improved?

- Has faith risen in your heart?

- Do you believe He is for you?

- Do you want to go even deeper?

The next set of 10 days are going to go much deeper. If you have yet to make the decision to accept Jesus into your heart, I hope these first 10 days have given you a good picture of Him: outside of how He is displayed by the majority of the world, but how the Word of God describes Him. There is no other relationship like Jesus. Salvation is a simple process yet it means everything. You believe in your heart and confess with your mouth that Jesus Christ is Lord. Here is a prayer you can use but you do not have to. You can make up your own. The important thing is, that you are sincere in your heart. Once you accept Jesus, if I never meet you or hear from you, then I'll see you in Heaven!

"Heavenly Father, I thank You for sending Jesus to save me from all sin. I believe that He is the Son of God, born of a virgin, lived a sinless life, was crucified on the cross, rose again three days later, ascended into Heaven, and someday is coming back to take His church home. I believe that I have received salvation now. I believe that my heart is now able to hear Your voice and to have a personal relationship with You. I am now a new creation in Jesus, and I am righteous in my spirit forevermore. Nothing can separate me from Your love, Jesus! I believe that now with salvation comes healing for my body and soul. I receive all the benefits of salvation in Jesus' name. Thank you Jesus for loving me! Amen!"

Days 11-20

Up to your knees

You are being challenged to go deeper. The teachings and poetry will awaken a fervent desire in your heart for the Lord. You shall be transformed as you continue to wade into Him. Your thoughts and meditations will be questioned. You may experience things you never thought possible. Your innermost desires will come to the surface. You shall experience the Lord at a whole new level.

Day 11

Taste and See

***Oh, taste and see that the LORD is good;
blessed is the man who trusts in Him! - Psalms
34:8 NKJV***

Taste and see that the Lord is good! Jesus has become our bread (body broken for us: sustenance, provision) and wine (blood of Christ shed for remission of sins: righteousness of God traded for our unrighteousness). Partake of Jesus! Come into union with Him.

We feed on the Word; He is our comfort! We can find our peace and rest by feeding, meditating, reading, and studying the Word of God! Whenever you need Him; He is available and free. You will want more Word once you get a taste.

We do not have to beg to be fed. We can feed ourselves with the Word of God. We used to have to wait on the rain: someone from the Levitical priesthood had to teach us. We had to wait for the right time: we could not approach the Holiest of holies. But now, because of Jesus, He has made us acceptable to God, and an eternal spring is in us. We learn from the Holy Spirit inside of us: whenever we desire! Taste and see that the Word is good!

Night 11

Come to My Table

I have set the table
I've prepared all of your favorites
I know just what you like
I've made this all for you
I won't allow an enemy to take even one bite
I won't let anyone bother us
You're safe here with Me

Partake here with Me
I want to enjoy your presence
I want to hear all about you
Your thoughts, desires and dreams
Your needs. wants, and memories
Confide in Me to your heart's content
I'm here to comfort you

Come to My table
Bring your worries, cares, and problems
Exchange them for peace, joy, and love
You're always welcome here
My beloved child

Day 12

Feed on Jesus

And Jesus said to them, "I Am the Bread of Life. He who comes to Me shall never hunger, and he who believes in Me shall never thirst." - John 6:15 NKJV

You are what you think. You are what you eat (what you meditate on). What are you feeding your soul? The Word of God is the only true satisfaction our souls need. Jesus is the Bread and Water of Life. He sustains us. He is our nutrition. Everything else is empty calories but Jesus gives us full energy.

Think on His Word. Train your soul's appetite to feed on the Word of God first. Do not stress eat worldly things but find your peace feeding on the Word of God. Do not gain unnecessary soul weight. For Jesus' burden is light and easy to bear. Extra weight will hold you back in worry and fear. Exercise your soul to give all cares to Jesus and stay healthy. Trust in His love; it will keep you in good shape!

Night 12

Thanks to Your Love

I know that You love me
I believe that You care for me
My surroundings may change
But You never will

My needs are always met
By Your abundant grace
No thing can take Your place
My faith is confident in Your Word

What should I worry about?
You are fighting on my side
No fear can shake me off the Rock
No weapon can pierce the armor of God

No enemy can snatch me from Your hand
I am more than a conqueror
Because of what You've done for me
All thanks to Your love

Day 13

Spring Restored

"But whoever drinks of the water that I shall give him will never thirst. But the water that I shall give him will become in him a fountain of water springing up into everlasting life." -
John 4:14 NKJV

Before the flood, water would spring forth from underground to water the plants and trees. It was perfect as God intended. There was no waiting for rain. Everything needed was provided.

After the flood, they had to now get used to rain. Rain was required and only came in intervals. Water was no longer as plentiful as it had been. They lived in a desert. If they did not get water at the right times, their crops would die out.

Jesus restored the spring to us! He is inside of us. He springs up from our spirit and waters our soul and body while healing and providing for it. We do not have to wait for the rain. We are given everything that we need. It is in us now! Draw from the Well of Salvation, Jesus!

Night 13

Open Vessel

I'm an open vessel
I hear the abundance of rain
I'll receive as much as I can
This is just a small portion

Much more is available
I'm already overflowing
Your goodness is relentless
Your love is boundless

Your promises flood me
I must share so I can receive more
I pour out what You've given me
To save the thirsty ones

I'll show them the source
Where living water runs freely
Where the waterfalls of blessing are
Where streams of grace flow

There's no limit to Your mercy
Endless provision for all Your children
We've taken the lids off our hearts
We're open vessels

Day 14

Receive from the Table of Promises

6 So He commanded the multitude to sit down on the ground. and He took the seven loaves and gave thanks, broke them and gave them to His disciples to set before them; and they set them before the multitude. 7 They also had a few small fish; and having blessed them, He said to set them also before them. 8 So they ate and were filled, and they took up seven large baskets of leftover fragments. - Mark 8:6-8 NKJV

Jesus was the Bread that was broken for us and multiplied to share His life with us.

All the food was laid out in front of them. The people had to take the food: make a conscious decision to partake of what was in front of them. Everything has been prepared for us! We need to eat, drink, be joyful, and thankful to God for setting His love on us! It is our responsibility to receive the promises of God. We take them in faith, and proclaim them until our heart understands the promise is more real than the circumstance.

Our cup runs over because there is an everlasting supply. We can have as much as we want!

Jesus paid the price for our health and prosperity. In fact, He overpaid by so much that there is no comparison, no scale or measurement, that can compare sin to grace. Jesus broke the bank. He set a new standard: a limitless supply!

Eat of His body, knowing that the work is finished and that every promise is ready for you to take. Drink of His blood, knowing that the redemption of sin is a done deal and that you are righteous. Receive whatever you need today from His bountiful table of promises!

Night 14

Run to Your Table

I run to Your table
I desire to dine with You
Break the bread
Pour the wine
I've cleared my schedule
I want to spend time with You

Jesus, precious Lamb of God
Your body was broken for me
Your blood poured out to wash me clean
I honor You my Saving Grace
All I can say is thank You
Let's dine together, today

I run to Your throne room
I desire to meet with You
I've brought all my cares
Your Grace is more than enough for me
I've stopped worrying about life
I know it'll work out in my favor

Giver of Mercy and Grace
You suffered judgment so I wouldn't have to
You sought out and found me

You'll never let me go
I take on Your yoke
We'll travel together, forever

Day 15

Sun of Righteousness

But to you who fear My name the Sun of Righteousness shall arise with healing in His wings; and you shall go out and grow fat like stall-fed calves. - Malachi 4:2 NKJV

His light energizes us. We become brighter and shine longer. If you disconnect from the sun, the power source, it will become dark.

Get closer to the Son of Righteousness! Become a blinding light of Jesus' warmth. Become a shining beacon of hope. Become a banisher of darkness.

Study His Word, meditate on His goodness, and spend time with Him. As you spend time in His presence, you will intrinsically store His light. You will not be able to suppress His love that exudes from you!

Night 15

Universe of Love

Love the Binding Force
Holds the universe together
Gathers all the planets and stars
Strings them together as a celestial strand of light
Wraps them about in twinkling beauty
Displays them across the night sky

Love the Great Attractor
Pulls us into Its orbit
Never lets us go
Safely places us in Its care
Shines Its light and dispels our darkness
Gives us energy to grow and live

Love the Compassionate Caregiver
Brings us protection
Redirects things that would strike us
Brings us warmth
Clothes us in an atmosphere of mercy
Creates good works in us

Love the Joy of My Countenance
Has called my name
Chosen me for such a time as this
Picked me up

Equipped me with favor
Supports me with grace

Love the Redeemer of My Heart
You found me deserted, barren, and dry
You restored me with the Waters of Life
Your springs burst forth in me
You breathed Your Spirit into me
You have revived my life

Day 16

Starlight

So when Jesus had received the sour wine, He said, "It is finished!" And bowing His head, He gave up His spirit. - John 19:30 NKJV

It can take light from the stars 100's of years to reach us, meaning that we are observing the star as it was that many years ago. If one was to go supernova we would not know until the light from the explosion reaches us. From where we are standing it looks like nothing has changed. However, because of how far it is, it could have undergone major changes. If you did not know it was far, you would think nothing is happening. We are watching what already happened in the past.

Let us compare to Jesus. From where we are standing, we can look back and read about His finished work. We can look back and read His Word to see healing, prosperity, and wisdom released. We can see it already done in the Bible. It happened so far in the past but we can see its effects now. How long it takes your heart to believe determines when the manifestation is received by you.

Light years - how far something has traveled at the speed of light in a year.
Word years - how far the Word of God has penetrated into your heart.

How many Word years will it take for you to receive? That is dependent on your relationship with God. The more you spend time in the Word and treasure His presence over the things of the world: you will start to change. Your mind will be renewed to His will and you will experience life anew.

You have to put some work into a relationship. You have to choose to spend time with that individual. You have to choose to get to know their likes and dislikes. Your heart is not fooled; you will not trust someone you do not know. If you take time to read and study the Bible, pray in the Spirit, and converse with God: you will experience transformation. It's impossible not to!

Night 16

Cosmic Painter

Let there be light
A burst of inspiration
In an instant the universe appeared
Woven in a tapestry of phantasmic fidelity
Held together by the vibration of Your voice

Cosmic Painter, You dotted the expanse
With entities small and big
Mixing the colors as You brushed across space

Galaxies added character
Blackholes for contrast
Quasars for impact
Not a one is exactly the same
You're always doing a new thing
You enjoy creating beauty

Space dust and clouds for that sparkle
Comets and Asteroids for texture
So many things and yet we're still discovering the scale of
your artistry

Ordered them in perfect fashion
Unbreakable limits and invisible paths they trace until
they are no more

Then they supernova, releasing the light that created them
in brilliant fireworks of celestial array
Then You form them again but this time a different way
You rearrange space and expand the astronomical canvas
even further

You constantly build upon what You've started
A miraculous engine of infinite proportion
How can we fathom such boundless creativity?
He thought all this up to show us His care
He's shared His love without compare

The One who set the Sun in the sky
The One who causes the moon to rise
The One who loves to Create
Has set His heart on humankind
Look up and see all that He's done
Starry nights are for us to enjoy

Day 17

Trust Him

4 Delight yourself also in the LORD, and He shall give you the desires of your heart. 5 Commit your way to the LORD, trust also in Him, and He shall bring it to pass. - Psalms 37:4-5 NKJV

There are times when we take on too much. We get full of ourselves. We think we can do it by our self. We get cocky. "That is okay God, I got this!" We tell ourselves we are strong enough, smart enough, and good enough to get by without His help.

God lets us do what we want. We have freewill to make decisions. He will honor your choice, whether it is good for you or not. We can make our lives exceedingly difficult when we get out of the spirit. When you try to do it yourself: you walk according to the lust of the flesh. You have taken off the yoke of Jesus and have put on the yoke of burden.

More often than not, we fail, fall down, condemn self, hurt our self or others, lose things, stress ourselves out, misuse finances, and waste time. When we have come to the point where we need God's intervention, we come to God asking for forgiveness. He is just to forgive us and help us. Oh, how much easier it would have been had we relied on

God first! We are going to end up relying on Him in the end anyway!

The desire you had could have been good, but when touched by fleshly lusts it was corrupted. God will renew and refresh your dreams and desires as you draw near to Him. He has a better way for you to follow. An easier path. A safer path. A more prosperous path.

Trust in Him! Do not give up your dreams and desires! He will make it all work out and will turn around all the wasted time and resources into a beautiful masterpiece of grace!

Night 17

Dream

I used to think I was alone on an island, never needing any-
one
But then You broke into my life and saved me from myself
I had big dreams but never knew how I would get there
Didn't even know where they came from
But now I know that You were guiding me to where you
wanted me to be

So I'll dream bigger
I'll believe stronger
I know that You are with me
I can do anything through You
So take these desires
Mold them into reality
I surrender my control
I can see pictures of my future
I know that You'll lead me there
Have Your way, Lord
With these dreams

Day 18

Automatic Updates

Blessed be the Lord, Who daily loads us with benefits, the God of our salvation! Selah - Psalms 68:19 NKJV

Many do not like automatic updates because they break existing functionality or remove features of our phones, tablets, and computers. You were either given no choice or it was updated overnight. How many times has your system crashed because you were forced into updating?

It is an exceedingly good thing that Jesus does perfect updates. When He updates us, we do not lose functionality or features! He daily loads us with grace, mercy, love, peace, joy, patience, goodness, kindness, meekness, wisdom and all goodness.

There are times when we need an adjustment that only our Administrator can perform. He corrects, repairs, and upgrades us. He is the Server; we are the workstations. He is not finished with us. He will keep working on our operating system (soul) as long as we keep our connection to Him.

Read the Bible and spend time with God. He'll upgrade your operating system automatically and perfectly!

Night 18

Not a Wretch

The old has faded away
My desires are Yours to mold
Freedom reigns in me
No longer bound by sin
My Spirit now one with Yours
My mind daily renewed

You made me new
Transformed my heart of stone
You made me new
Jesus my Cornerstone the Rock of My Salvation
You made me new
Called me from the darkness into Your loving light
Forever changed into the image of You
You made me new

No longer am I a wretch
I'm the righteousness of God in Christ Jesus
No longer am I estranged from life
You picked me up when I was down
You set my feet on solid ground
You gave me a home and gave me Your name
I'm forever new and seated with Christ above

Day 19

Believe God

"A good man out of the good treasure of his heart brings forth good; and an evil man out of the evil treasure of his heart brings forth evil. For out of the abundance of the heart his mouth speaks." - Luke 6:45 NKJV

Knowing something does not impact you as much, unless, you believe it. What you believe will define who you are. What you believe is written on your heart. What you know can change; what you believe is not as volatile.

It can be difficult to reach someone who believes something contrary to Jesus. They have written something on their heart that makes them shy away from Jesus. There is a reason we call it, "belief system," and not, "fact system." Facts do not direct our way of life like beliefs do.

It is vitally important to believe what God has said over any, "fact." When our beliefs line up with the Word of God, our faith is empowered. We speak forth what we believe, in expectation, to bring it out of our spirit into this reality. Choose to believe what God has said over any other word!

Night 19

He's Got This

Who are you?
I see you in the mirror.
But I don't recognize you.
At one time, I may have known you.
But those days are long past.

How long ago has it really been?
This visage staring back at me, why are you depressed?
Where is the joy that used to exude through your smile?
Where is the peace that showed through your posture?
Where is the life that glinted in your eyes?

What have you been doing?
What have you been watching?
What have you been listening to?
You are missing something.
You are trying too hard.

Why have you let the world weigh you down with their troubles?
Why have you let their worries become your own?
Why have you not relied on Jesus, the One who carries your burdens?
Did you think you could live by yourself?
Did you honestly believe you were better off alone?

My soul why are you downtrodden?
Hope in God!
Remember His victories.
This shall be a testimony to His goodness.
What Satan meant for evil will be turned around for good.

Don't buy into the lies of Satan.
Don't believe a thing he has said.
Return to your First Love.
There's still time to turn around.
You will overcome this.

Your joy shall be restored.
Your peace shall increase.
Your life will get better.
You will cast off the spirit of heaviness and put on the garment of praise.
You will triumph in victory.

You are not alone.
Jesus is with you.
He shall strengthen you.
His Word stands firm.
He watches over to perform it.

Raise your head high!
Put on that smile, we've come to know.
Walk in confidence, knowing it's finished.
Stare boldly toward the future.
You've got this because He's got this.

Day 20

Christ Is Your Faith

So then faith comes by hearing, and hearing by the word of God. - Romans 10:17 NKJV

We were given the full measure of faith when we believed in Jesus. It is His faith working in us! Faith is activated by the Word of God. The more you hear the Word, the more your faith is activated. When faith is activated, it can be used to accomplish amazing things through the Holy Spirit such as healings, miracles, prophecies, words of knowledge, and words of wisdom. Jesus grew in wisdom and activated His faith which allowed Him to walk in such authority.

Take time to activate your faith. Study to show yourself that you are loved by God. You aren't ashamed anymore. Jesus took all condemnation and buried it in the grave. You can rightly discern the Word of Truth because the Holy Spirit is teaching you.

Believe what God has said about you! Trust in His unfailing faithfulness. Your faith is strong because His is strong. Unbelief has no chance in your heart. Fear has no place to rest in your mind. You can do all things through Christ: Who is Your Faith!

Night 20

Why?

Why should I be surprised,
When what I pray for happens?
Why should I be surprised,
When a miracle occurs in front of me?
Why should I be surprised,
When the mountain jumps into the sea?

This should be normal,
For a Christian walk.

This is the power of Christ in me.
This is the evergiving flow of life.
He pours out of me.
This same Spirit that raised Jesus from the dead.
He has decided to dwell in me.

Healings, miracles, and breakthroughs,
Should be commonplace.
I will expect it more.
I won't be surprised anymore.

Review Days 11-20

Baptism of the Holy Spirit

Overflow of your wineskin: gushing forth with power

We are wading deeper now.

- How are you enjoying the revelations?

- Are the days and nights speaking to you?

- What are you learning?

- What has changed in your thinking?

- Have you noticed changes in your heart?

We are getting to the meat of the book. We are going to talk about deep revelations. To take advantage of the rest of the book, you should be baptized in the Holy Spirit.

I can honestly tell you, that the Baptism of the Holy Spirit absolutely transformed my life. My passion for things of God grew exponentially. I could not read the Word enough. The Bible became alive to me. The Holy Spirit would speak to me about what I was reading. I could have conversations with God and hear His voice so clearly. A passion for music formed inside of me and now it is a vital part of my ministry. Speaking in tongues brings me peace like no other and also a presence of God that overwhelms. I would not be song writing, book writing, playing and singing music, ministering, and teaching the Word of God if it was not for the Baptism of the Holy Spirit. The Baptism of the Holy Spirit is a requirement to make an impact through the power of Jesus in this world!

If you have a real desire to go deeper with the Lord, you must make sure you are filled with the Holy Spirit to the overflow. Here is a prayer to receive the Baptism of the Holy Spirit with the evidence of speaking in tongues.

> *"Holy Spirit, I ask You to baptize and fill me right now. I desire to be a witness for Jesus and to be fully equipped in every good work. Holy Spirit, I thank You for infilling me and for awakening my heart to hear You more and to make the Word of God come alive in me as I read and study. Thank You Lord! I believe I have received you now! I now open my mouth, yield my tongue, and speak in my personal prayer language as the spirit gives me utterance." (Allow yourself to begin to speak as He gives you the words.)*

If you do not speak in tongues immediately, do not fret. It wasn't instant for me either. It took me about a week to manifest my prayer language. I was praising and worshiping the Lord in my room, and my words started changing to a different sound altogether! The hardest thing about tongues, is not thinking about it. Tongues come out of the spirit and not out of the mind. You speak but the

Holy Spirit will produce the syllables, sounds, and vocalizations. Do not give up! Keep trying! You asked so therefore you have received.

Days 21-30

Up to your heart

You are understanding the deep things of God. The Holy Spirit is leading you deeper into truth and revelation. Old things you believed are being washed away with the renewal of the Word. You are consciously seeking the Lord in your life. He is equipping you to live out His Word as a light in the darkness. You know who you are in Him. You have a firm grasp of His plans for you. His Word in you is producing fruitful results in your life.

Day 21

Take Him Out of the Box

"For with God nothing will be impossible." -
Luke 1:37 NKJV

Why are things put into a box? To protect yourself from
what is inside or to protect the contents from harm. When
you take God out of the box, you can expect these things
to happen.

- Fear of the unknown will be cast aside.

- You'll begin to trust Him more.

- Your faith will be strengthened.

- You will understand Him better.

- You can interact with Him more intimately.

He is the Gift inside the box. Take Him out! Experience
Him for yourself without limits!

Night 21

Letter to My Bride

To My dearest beloved,

How are you? I so long to be with you. I've been counting the moments until our ceremony. My Father is still preparing everything. He told Me not to worry. He'd take care of all the arrangements.

Did you receive My gifts? I had My messengers deliver them. I don't want you to lack any good thing. I sent my Advisor to assist you. He'll help prepare you for the wedding. He knows Me just as well as My Father. I'm sure He will comfort you until I return.

I also sent you a fruit basket. I handpicked each one Myself: making sure each one would give you vital nutrition to sustain you. They are the same ones that I partake. Please help yourself. I wouldn't want you to go hungry. Please freely eat as often as you'd like.

Your dress is coming along nicely. It is so breathtakingly beautiful but it pales in comparison to My spotless bride. The jewels that adorn it make it twinkle like the cloudless night sky.

Your veil is being knitted from the finest silk in all the Kingdom. It is dainty and translucent like a rich ivory yet it allows light in to reflect the color of your eyes.

Your crown is being molded from the purest gold. My Father Himself carefully chose each piece from His own treasury. He loves you as much as I do! He is excited to welcome you into Our family.

You have to see this house my Father built for us! It will accommodate our every need. It has been furnished with the most beautiful furniture, the most vibrant colors and more than enough room for us to share. It's overflowing in abundance and extravagance. Words can't fully describe its magnificent splendor.

My soon-to-be betrothed, how I dearly love you! I can't stop thinking about you. I want to always be by your side. I want to feel the warmth of your embrace. I want to feel the passion of your kisses. I want to be captivated by your comeliness. I want to hold your hand and walk through eternity with you. Oh, how I long for you My perfect bride!

My beloved, please wait just a bit longer. I know you long for Me as well. I have business that must be attended to. If I could be there now I would. Until then, I'll remember that each breath is one breath closer to you. I'll be the perfect Groom for you. Even though I can't be with you yet, if you ever need anything ask my Advisor and He will reach Me. I will take care of you for all eternity.

With all of Love's blessings,

Your Bridegroom forever,

Jesus Christ

Day 22

God Wants You Free

It shall come to pass in that day that his burden will be taken away from your shoulder, and his yoke from your neck, and the yoke will be destroyed because of the anointing oil. - Isaiah 10:27 NKJV

The anointing breaks the yoke! Yokes go over the animal's neck. The neck controls the head. We used to be yoked to sin. Being a slave means you could not make your own path. You could not direct your own steps. You would have no control over where you would go.

God wants you free so you can experience life! The anointing is indicative of the Holy Spirit. You have been sanctified by the Holy Spirit; your true nature is holy and righteous! You are the dwelling place for God! Because God dwells in you, you are free.

We are anointed by God to be ministers. Ministry doesn't mean pulpit ministry, but that everywhere we go, we manifest God's love and are open to being His voice, His hands, and His feet. God wants you free so that you can show the world that He is good. God has set you free, so you can set others free! You are free from the yoke of bondage; you can proclaim the freedom of Jesus to everyone!

Night 22

Army of Christ

Salvation has made His way to us
We've been set free from our prisons
We are the army of Christ

We must tell someone about our Lord
His great incredible love
We are the army of Christ

We will carry Your name in all the Earth
We are flag bearers of Your love
We are the army of Christ

Equipped with a sword that can cut through lies
We bring the Truth to the masses
We are the army of Christ

Shield in hand that protects us
All flaming arrows shall be quenched
We are the army of Christ

We march toward the enemy's strongholds
Through Jesus we pull them down
We are the army of Christ

We're taking back the stolen ground
We have dominion everywhere we walk
We are the army of Christ

We raise a banner of Victory
No enemy can stand against us
We are the army of Christ

Day 23

Created in Joy

Then he said to them, "Go your way, eat the fat, drink the sweet, and send portions to those for whom nothing is prepared; for this day is holy to our Lord. Do not sorrow, for the joy of the LORD is your strength." - Nehemiah 8:10 NKJV

We were created in the joy of God. He had fun creating each of us with much laughter and joy. We are products of His joy. We are the joy of God. This is why the joy of the Lord is our strength. He created us with joy!

Joy accesses the creative ability of God to overcome any problem. Praise, worship, thanksgiving, relationship with God, prayer, fellowship with like-minded believers, and praying in tongues all feed our joy. We have an everlasting spring of joy in our spirit. As we get closer to the Creator we start to model our ways and thoughts after His!

He has fun creating, and so do we! All people are creative in their own way. We get joy out of creating things. Because our God gave us that same ability: to create in joy.

Night 23

Bubble

Gentle as a summer breeze
Pushed away by a little sneeze

Round and filled with hope
Could even be made out of soap

Breath of God in airy form
Can escape any storm

Promises of God made manifest
Can be seen close to your chest

Rise up high into the sky
Never looking down or asking why

Colors galore seen in the core
Beautiful and radiant forevermore

Reflects the light of the Son
Oh, how He loves to have fun

Look inside and see your future
Be surrounded by love so sure

Joy bubbles up from our spirit
Encouraging us to never quit

Here for an instant and gone in a flash
Can't be bought for any amount of cash

Our Father will keep us from trouble
Remember, life is precious and fragile like a bubble

Day 24

No More Thorns

And they clothed Him with purple; and they twisted a crown of thorns, put it on His head, -
Mark 15:17 NKJV

Thorns were considered a curse. The ground, at one time, was blessed. It used to be self-sufficient, but the fall of humankind cursed the ground with sin. Adam and all his descendants would have to toil in hard labor to bring forth a harvest. But Jesus came to restore the land too.

Jesus became a curse for us so that we could become the righteousness of God through Him. Jesus took all your thorny cares even though they caused you mental torment. The piercing pains of trauma, anxiety, fear and mental imbalances have all been taken away by Jesus!

The ground is no longer cursed with thorns and briars! You can have a bountiful harvest in Jesus! You can reap all the benefits of His promises because He exchanged all our curses for His blessings!

Night 24

Lord of the Seasons

The Lord of the Seasons
Has declared a blessing
Over all your fields and lands

He's bringing abundance
Increase is on the way
Plant your seeds

Build your storehouses
There's a Harvest coming
Make ready to receive

You won't be able to store it all
Give as much away as you want
Feed all the poor and hungry

Draw them in and teach disciples
Finance every good work
Build up the Kingdom of God

Showcase the goodness of Jesus
You have been made into a blessing
In every season you will prosper

Day 25

Guard Your Tongue

Let no corrupt word proceed out of your mouth, but what is good for necessary edification, that it may impart grace to the hearers. - Ephesians 4:29 NKJV

If you do not have anything good to say; do not say anything at all! Protect your tongue. Do not complain, do not speak negatively, and do not always speak what is on your mind.

Life and death are in the power of the tongue! Speak life. Speak the goodness of God. Speak the peace of God. Speak the blessings of God. Speak Jesus!

Do not curse others! Do not curse what God has blessed! Do not curse yourself! Do not allow any death to come out of your mouth. Only speak what God's Word says about you, others, and about Himself.

Night 25

Anthem of Praise

Anthems stream from people everywhere
Magnificent Jesus our Beloved Savior

Worship flows out of our hearts
Worthy Jesus all praise belongs to You

Thanksgiving rises from our lips
Awesome Jesus our Conquering King

Together we magnify Your Holy Name
Graceful Jesus Your splendor envelops all of creation

In one accord we lift our hearts to You
No one is more magnificent, worthy, awesome, and graceful than You our Lord of Love

Be Thou glorified in all the Earth

Day 26

Will of Jesus

Therefore it is of faith that it might be according to grace, so that the promise might be sure to all the seed, not only to those who are of the law, but also to those who are of the faith of Abraham, who is the father of us all. - Romans 4:16 NKJV

A written will does not come into effect until death. Jesus is able to be the executor of His will because He conquered death. He wrote down all that He left us: Healing, Prosperity, Purpose, Righteousness, Peace, Joy, and every good gift. We are the heirs; we have inherited from His will.

His will is for us. Dying and rising from the grave was the, 'seal,' on the document. It is a completed covenant. Jesus has distributed His unlimited riches to all His co-heirs. Any who would believe on His name is considered part of the family and can share in the family's wealth. He freely gave of Himself so you wouldn't lack any good thing. Believe on Jesus and take as much as you want!

Night 26

El Shaddai

El Shaddai
Endless supply
Never asking why

You're not shy
You keep Your eye
Watching from on high

Feeling spry
Ready to try
You want me to fly

My oh my
Into the sky
Leaving the ground by

I won't sigh
You will not lie
Won't lead me awry

You did tie
Myself to Thy
You won't let me die

Not goodbye
Just a short fly
So please do not cry

Here am I
Living on high
With my El Shaddai

Day 27

Kingdom of God

And if children, then heirs—heirs of God and joint heirs with Christ... - Romans 8:17 NKJV

We are co-equals with Jesus. One-third of us (spirit man) is 100% Him. We are seated with Him in Heaven above all. Jesus is like our older brother. He guides and helps us along as He teaches us the family business.

We are princes and princesses in the Kingdom of God. We are tasked with bringing the knowledge of our Kingdom to Earth. Through the power of the Holy Spirit we are able to do the same feats as Jesus. Healing and miracles were commonplace for Him. So as it should be with us.

We are an extension of the Kingdom and authority of God. We have been given the right to exert our Kingdom's authority as ambassadors of Grace. We declare what our Kingdom stands for and what is available to those who would believe. It is an open Kingdom of light, freedom, love, and prosperity. A Kingdom of which is unlike any in the world. We want to share the goodness of our Kingdom with every creature.

Satan is the usurper. He has pretended to be a king and many have fallen in his trap. He steals, kills, and destroys those who serve him. Only through the power of God can we rescue these tormented souls and bring them into our Kingdom where they will find freedom, healing, love, prosperity and peace.

Share the love and grace of Jesus. There are still many who do not know of the goodness of our Kingdom. Be moved with compassion just as Jesus was. Reach out today!

Night 27

Answer

I've been watching,
Observing from far away.
I see the hurt,
Injustice, and hate.
How long will I be here?
Watching and doing,
Absolutely nothing?

Jesus is the same today and forever.
His love never grows cold or distant.
He's reaching out through His hands and feet,
To share His goodness with any who would believe.
Jesus was sent to do the Father's will.
He transforms lives and erases evil.

Wake up my sleeping heart!
The time is now.
The world needs the Answer!
The sidelines are crowded.
It's time to step out and be the light.
To take a stand for what's right.

We'll lead people to the Answer!
The One who cares for them so.
We'll bring them to the King.

Who wants to restore them.
We'll demonstrate His Grace,
And they'll fall on their face.

Day 28

Demand the Promise

And if you are Christ's, then you are Abraham's seed, and heirs according to the promise. - Galatians 3:29 NKJV

Make a demand on the promise! God is looking for such as those to hold Him accountable. We have legal claim to the promises because we are children of God. We have inherited the blessings of the family. God is our Father. We've been grafted into Abraham's family through faith just as he was adopted into God's family by faith.

We are children of the promise; faith is our binding agent. Together in Christ, we have legal claim to the promises of God. Jesus fulfilled the Old Testament law which means all the blessings are His. We share in His victory by believing in His finished work. He lives on the inside of us. We access the promises through Jesus.

Make a demand on the promise! Ask and you shall receive if you do not disbelieve. God is not withholding anything from you. Demand the promise, visualize it, speak it forth, and see it happen!

Night 28

Thrive

Thrive don't strive
Live don't die
Love don't hate
Receive don't reject
Be don't do
Trust don't feel
Hope don't worry
Believe don't doubt
Win don't lose

Bold not shy
Confident not fearful
Powerful not weak
Peaceful not emotional
Joyful not depressed
Excited not bored
Merciful not judgmental
Thankful not prideful
Jesus not world

Day 29

Why Are You Waiting?

Let us therefore come boldly to the throne of Grace, that we may obtain mercy and find Grace to help in time of need. - Hebrews 4:16 NKJV

What are you waiting for? You can skip the line! You have an open appointment with the King. You can come and go as you please. You are His child. His kingdom is your kingdom. You can share the same things. You can have what He has.

Come boldly to the throne of Grace and receive whatever you need. His Grace is provision for you. Activate your faith by speaking the Word of God confidently. God's not holding out on you. So what are you waiting for?

Night 29

Waiting

You were waiting on me,
To fully trust You.

You were waiting on me,
To let go and cast it on You.

You were waiting on me,
To start resting so You could work.

You were waiting on me,
To stay my hand from it.

You were waiting on me,
To speak out in authority.

You were waiting on me,
To thank You for the victory.

You were waiting on me,
At Your table of grace.

You were waiting on me,
To serve me Your blessings.

You were waiting on me,
To provide my every need.

You were waiting on me,
To taste and see Your goodness.

You were waiting on me,
To comfort my heart.

You were waiting on me,
To hold me in Your embrace.

Day 30

Victory Is Yours

For all the promises of God in Him are Yes, and in Him Amen, to the glory of God through us. - 2 Corinthians 1:20 NKJV

The deed has been signed. The title is ready for you to pick up. Victory is yours if you will take hold of it.

Healing has been signed over to you. Prosperity is waiting for you. Will you go and accept it?

Every promise has been signed over in Jesus' name. The fine print is real short. It just says "Yes!" Will you boldly enter the throne room and take it? Will you make a demand on the promise and receive what is yours?

Open your mouth and receive with authority! Receive with thanksgiving! Take possession of the promises today! They have your name on it!

Night 30

I AM

I AM accepted
He has taken my shame

I AM redeemed
He has erased my sin

I AM special
He has made me unique

I AM blessed
He has gifted me with grace

I AM called
He has equipped me with goodness

I AM beloved
He enjoys me

I AM protected
He cares for me

I AM victorious
He reigns through me

I AM complete
He has restored me

I AM His
He knows me

Review Days 21-30

Consecration

Fermenting the wine: aging of the vintage

Your journey is progressing!

- Have you noticed a change in your walk with God?

- Do you believe you have drawn closer?

- Do you hear His voice and follow His guidance more often?

- Has He been teaching you all sorts of things?

- What habits of yours have changed?

When we take the time to focus on God's Word and meditate on His precepts, we shall change. There is no maybe or if. The Word of God is a transformational, all-powerful, and life-giving force that makes an impact when it is read, understood, believed and proclaimed. Would you like to go even deeper?

Consecration is the process of being set apart. It's a full dedication to the Lord. The priests of yore had to be consecrated to serve before God in the temple and before the Ark of the Covenant. It required a set of specific rituals that we can see as a shadow of the spiritual. The anointing oil is the Holy Spirit. In Acts, Paul and Barnabas were set apart by the Holy Spirit for their purpose in ministry. Consecration is an important part of our relationship with God. Here's an example prayer that you can use to consecrate yourself to the Lord.

"Lord Jesus, I thank You for Your influence in my life. Lord, I vow to only ever follow You. I devote my entire life, hopes, dreams, talents, abilities, giftings, desires, and passions to You. Have Your way in my life. I open my heart to Your correction, discipline and cleansing by fire. Lord, reveal to me whatever is in my heart that is not of You. I denounce any sort of sin, unforgiveness, unhealthy habits and anything else that does not bring glory to Your name. I thank You Jesus, for showing me the path of Grace to walk upon. I follow You lord, all the days of my life because You are My Delight. In Jesus' name I commit myself to You. Amen."

Days 31-40

Over your head

You have dove completely into the Lord. You are no longer relying on your strength but His. He has transformed your thinking and you have clarity in your life. He is helping you to be all that He has called you to be. He speaks, you listen, and you obey. He can trust you to carry out His will on the Earth. You are surrendered completely to Him. You are being raised up to set the captives free, to heal the sick, to cleanse the lepers, bring the dead to life, and to cast out demons. Signs and wonders follow you because you have put your trust in Jesus' Word!

Day 31

Faith Produces an Action

Then I said, "I will not make mention of Him, nor speak anymore in His name." But His word was in my heart like a burning fire shut up in my bones; I was weary of holding it back, and I could not. - Jeremiah 20:9 NKJV

Faith without action is not faith. Faith produces an action. Speaking is an action.

Staying silent is inaction. Faith requires an action to make it faith. Hope does not require action. Hope is a confident expectation of good. Hope looks toward the future not to the present. Many people are hoping but not believing. Believing is done with the heart; hoping is done with the mind.

Hoping is good, it comes before faith. But, if it is left in the mind, it will not mature into belief. Meditating and declaring the Word of God, spending time with God, fellowshipping with like-minded believers, and worship, are some ways we can transform hope into belief. Then belief will naturally lead into an action of faith.

Night 31

I Thank You

To whom do I owe everything?
To whom belongs the praise?

It's a simple thing to say thank You.
It's a different thing entirely to live out.

Memories flood my mind.
Memories full of goodness.

My life poured out in offering.
My life surrendered in thanksgiving.

All things are possible to Him who believes.
All things are possible to us except to thank You enough.

Every breath well-spent on worship.
Every breath streams forth hallelujah.

I step into Your throne room.
I step closer to adore and honor You.

I fall down to my knees and cry out, "Worthy!"
I fall down on my face and proclaim, "Holy!"

Thank You God for being You.
Thank You God for allowing me to experience Your love.

Eternally grateful to You my True Love.
Eternally grateful that You called my name.

Forever isn't long enough.
Forever barely scratches the surface.

I'll praise You with my lips.
I'll praise You with my dance.

I will thank You always.
I will thank You even now.

I thank You.
I thank You.

Day 32

We Cannot Be Separated

38 For I am persuaded that neither death nor life, nor angels nor principalities nor powers, nor things present nor things to come, 39 nor height nor depth, nor any other created thing, shall be able to separate us from the love of God which is in Christ Jesus our Lord. - Romans 8:38-39 NKJV

Since you cannot be separated from His love: You cannot be separated from His healing!

There are no, "levels," of healing. It is as easy for God to heal a splinter as it is for Him to grow out a limb. It is the same power that worked in Jesus that would heal both of these.

Our faith should not be affected by the circumstances. Life or death situations can have a serious impact on emotions. Unbelief can flourish in dire circumstances. This is where our soul tries to get us to stop trusting and start doubting. There is no room for doubt for those that believe. Do not allow a door of fear to allow doubt to make a room in your mind. Leave no place for Satan to roam!

Quote the Word of God and stand on it with full assurance. Trust that He is faithful to complete or perfect His Word in any situation it is brought into. His Word does not return void but shall accomplish His will. Thank Him for the desired result now. Thank Him for the answered prayer, manifested healing, or powerful wisdom now!

Faith is now, it is active, and dynamic. Faith moves mountains out of the way and splits oceans in half. Faith allows us to access all the benefits Grace has provided. Healing is part of salvation. Jesus took stripes on His back to give us healing. The Holy Spirit in us quickens our mortal body to receive healing. Healing is already in our spirit; we need to activate it by speaking forth God's Word!

Night 32

I Am Supernatural

I refuse to be normal
I won't conform to their standard
I am a new creation
Gone is my old self
I am supernatural

Sickness is not for me
Disease has no right
Sin has been dealt with
Praise God I'm reborn
I am supernatural

I am a creature of Grace and my home is in Heaven
I am a spirit being and I am perfect
The same Spirit that raised Jesus from the dead is in me
I live through faith and am empowered by Christ
I am supernatural

Circumstances don't dictate what I believe
Your Word is supernatural
It dwells deep within me
Dynamic power flows out of my spirit
I am supernatural

Miracles are natural because Your Spirit does the work
I trust in Your unfailing kindness and healing Grace
You enable me to live above a fleshly life
All things are possible because I believe
I am supernatural

Day 33

Downloading From God

"Ask, and it will be given to you; seek, and you will find; knock, and it will be opened to you."
- Matthew 7:7 NKJV

Receiving from God can be compared to downloading a file.

- Choose your file to download. This is choosing a promise to believe on. You will want to know what the software does. You will want a clear picture of what the promise will look like operating in your life. The file size is dependent on what the app does. You could be downloading a 4 KB installer (small) or a 2 GB archive (large). Some promises of God seem bigger and more difficult to receive. It is all about your perspective. The only thing that will hold you back is your thinking.

- Files are downloaded in pieces. The network and the file server determine the speed at which it downloads. Believing increases speed, and reducing doubt increases throughput. The server is our spirit. It contains all the data we need. Our communication to the server is the faith of Jesus. That is how we fetch the data from our server.

- The file is unrecognizable until it is fully downloaded. When all the pieces have been received; it is put together and able to be used. Many times it looks like nothing is happening on the surface. If you do not have a progress bar to see, then you may come to the conclusion that it did not work. However, things are happening in the background. You are receiving from God. Your faith is being perfected in Jesus. You are learning to trust and rely upon Him. Patience is the ability to receive in faith: the process of faith working.

- Now that the file is complete: you can install it. This is the process of speaking it forth and pulling it out into the natural. Install the promise into your body. Reap the benefits of the promise.

- Open source software is supported by donors. People who are thankful to the developers give time and money to show they support their work. When we are thankful to God for His promise; it opens up a desire to give back to Him. We donate our gifts, talents, finances and love to show our support to Jesus. He freely provided all our needs. He did not leave anything out. He did it all for free.

Receiving from God is a simple process. Choose what to believe for (get a clear picture in your mind), remove all doubt (trust in His love), speak the promise forth (see it manifest in the natural), and thank Him for it (give Him praise).

Night 33

I'll Never Find Out

What would I do without You?
I'm glad, I'll never find out.
Life without hope is no life at all.
Thank You for not giving up on me.
Even in the midst of the storm,
You were right there calming the wind.
You wouldn't let me drown.
You lifted me up to walk on water with You.
Waves are no match for Grace.

What would I do without You?
I'm glad, I'll never find out.
When the armies of Satan rushed toward me,
You jumped right in and protected me.
You shined Your light and they ran far away.
You gave me Your armor and lent me Your sword.
You instructed me in righteousness.
You taught me to fight and now no enemy can stand against.
Darkness has no chance against Grace.

What would I do without you?
I'm glad, I'll never find out.
When circumstances tried to overtake me,
Your joy rose up in my heart.

I cried out with a song of praise.
Thanksgiving and worship poured from my lips.
My attitude changed as I focused on Your goodness.
My mountain grew smaller as I magnified You.
Mountains collapse in the presence of Grace.

What would I do without You?
I'm glad, I'll never find out.
I have so many testimonies of Your faithfulness to me.
I appreciate what You've done for me.
My paths drip with abundance.
My storehouses are overflowing.
My family is blessed and prosperous.
I've heard Your call and I've chosen to follow You.
Grace keeps me, leads me, and loves me.

What would I do without You?
I'm glad, I'll never find out!

Day 34

Jesus' Fire

"But you shall receive power when the Holy Spirit has come upon you; and you shall be witnesses to Me in Jerusalem, and in all Judea and Samaria, and to the end of the earth." - Acts 1:8 NKJV

We have the stronger fire! The purifying eternal flame of passionate love; the Holy Spirit dwells in us. Once you have received the Holy Spirit's baptism, you can be a witness to and for the power of God.

We have been given powerful spiritual gifts to pull down strongholds and take down evil's influence in the world. The fire of the Holy Spirit burns brightly and hotly. We have been given the privilege of sustaining a burning fire within us. The Holy Spirit empowers us to overtake Satan in every aspect. He consumes evil and melts every chain to set captives free. He also helps purify us by burning out every impurity found in our vessels. His fire will never grow cold, will never go out, and will never lose its intensity!

Hell's fire is one of fear, judgment, torment, and hate. Jesus' fire is one of acceptance, righteousness, and love. You will snuff out Hell's fire everywhere you go! Greater is the fire of the Holy Spirit that is housed in you than the enemy's fire that is burning in the world!

Night 34

Paid the Price

Every single life, Jesus paid the price
We've been given the order to find
Every child buried beneath the grime
Sin has no place to rest his head
Jesus made sure to kill him dead

The world is full of treasure
Each precious soul atoned for
Jesus values every one
He thought of you before it was done
Your freedom motivated Him and then He won

We're on a rescue mission
Letting people know
Jesus Christ loves them so
Breaking off their chains
And healing their pains

The Kingdom of Heaven is nigh
He lives within You and I
Our dominion is the Earth
Because we've been given new birth
Everywhere we go is a reason for mirth

So don't you worry and don't you fret
Let's all cast a vast and wide net
Compassion compels us, love is bold
Let's all tear down every stronghold
We'll send Satan packing and take back His gold

Day 35

Rely On Your Shepherd

"And when he brings out his own sheep, he goes before them; and the sheep follow him, for they know his voice." - John 10:4 NKJV

Learn to rely on the Holy Spirit all the time, not just when you are in trouble. He will prevent you from getting into trouble in the first place! That still small voice that sounds like you: that is what you need to listen for.

Quiet your own thoughts, meditate on the Lord, and expect to hear Him speak. We are His sheep and so we can hear our Shepherd's voice! Be assured, He is speaking to you.

If you cannot distinguish His voice from your own, then serve someone unseen. The flesh hates to serve and it really hates it when it is unseen. You will quiet the voice of the flesh and hear His voice clearly.

Be obedient to what He tells you. You will grow accustomed to hearing His voice and will distinguish it from your own the more you choose to act on what He says. Do not worry about getting it wrong, try anyway, His Grace covers all. It is better to try and get it wrong than to not try at all!

Night 35

Tarry

Just a little longer
Tarry with Me

I enjoy our time together
I cherish each moment
Forget Me not
I'm always thinking of you

Let Me show you My ways
I have secrets I want to share with you
Lie down with Me
Rest in My presence

Let Me heal your wounds
And take your pain
My desire is for You
I enjoy blessing you

You are My beloved child
I'll always be with you
To hold your hand
And comfort you

Don't neglect Me

For your name is written on My heart
I'll protect and defend you
I have set My angels to watch over you

Tell Me your fears
So I can wipe them away
I'll prove My love is for you
However long it takes

So tarry with Me
Just a little longer

Day 36

Answer the Phone

Now the Lord spoke to Paul in the night by a vision, "Do not be afraid, but speak, and do not keep silent;" - Acts 18:9 NKJV

The Holy Spirit will prompt us to give words of encouragement to people. We are the vessels that God communicates through to others. I liken it to a phone that rings. You have a ringing phone go off on the inside of you. You know God wants to reach out to the person but you ignore the phone. It keeps ringing and getting louder and eventually it becomes an irritant.

To get the phone to stop ringing you either unplug it or answer it. Unplugging it is hardening your heart to the voice of God. Answering it opens up God's voice to the person He wants to reach out to. The thing about the phone, you don't always know what the caller is going to say. Once we answer the phone, we can expect God to say what He has on His mind.

Earnestly seek to love others. Go out of your way to love people. Bless them, encourage them, and help them without them ever asking for it. Answer the phone: they need to hear what God wants to tell them!

Night 36

I Delight in You

I still remember the day.
As if it was a moment ago.
When I imagined you.
When I thought of your life.
Oh how it excites Me even now!

You were as My blank canvas.
I hand-sculpted your features and took My time crafting your face.
I painted you with the colors of Heaven.
You are My one-of-a-kind masterpiece.
I wouldn't change any detail about you; you were made perfect.

You turned out better than I could have hoped for!
I created you in expectation of all the fun we'd have together!
My eternally-loved child, how I cherish your presence.
The sweet sound of your voice is a magnificent melody to My ears.
Your outward affection makes My heart skip.

Your unique personality captivates Me.
I look forward to the decisions you make and the things you do.

I watch over your every step: making sure you don't slip or fall.
When you make a mistake: I'm always ready to catch you.
I'll clean you up and lead you along paths of Grace.

There's nothing I wouldn't do for you.
I'd give all of Heaven for you.
I sent My Son, Jesus to bring You home where you belong.
You are an important part of My family.
I could never replace you!

You encourage My heart.
What an honor to be the Father of you!
I'm grateful that you are Mine.
When you come to sit with Me: what joy fills My heart!
When you say My Name, My heart fills with ecstasy!

I enjoy blessing you.
I look forward to your radiant smile.
I have so many gifts to give you.
I won't let you lack any good thing.
I have supplied all your need.

Your dreams and desires are from Me.
Together, we'll fulfill them to the utmost!
I have planned amazing journeys for us.
As we walk together, I so adore your every move and breath.
I won't let anyone come between us.

You are a part of Me.
When I look into your gentle eyes, I see Me.
I'm greatly pleased with how you turned out.

It's My joy to instruct you in My ways.
You are Your Father's treasure.

I delight in you.

Day 37

Love is a Plus

11 And when the Pharisees saw it, they said to His disciples, "Why does your Teacher eat with tax collectors and sinners?" 12 When Jesus heard that, He said to them, "Those who are well have no need of a physician, but those who are sick. 13 But go and learn what this means: 'I desire mercy and not sacrifice. For I did not come to call the righteous, but sinners, to repentance.'" - Matthew 9:11-13 NKJV

Like a magnet, Jesus had compassion on people. He was attracted to where the sinners were. He desired them to be made well. In turn, the sinners knew they needed help and were attracted to the goodness and love of God.

Everyone has an attraction to love. Love is a plus. People know there is something missing in their life. They try to find the answer through all different mediums but only God can satisfy their hunger.

The cross was a giant plus sign to the world. The plus sign is the love and goodness of God.

The minus is when we fail to realize God is love and cares for us.

"— horizontal," caring about only people or yourself.

"| vertical," God caring for us.

"+," us caring for others through the love He's given us.

Be a plus in someone's life! Display the love of God to those you meet. You may be the catalyst for them to receive Christ.

Night 37

Love Is Eternity

From before time
You thought of the perfect place
Your breath created the perfect universe for us to inhabit
Your love expands faster than the fabric of the universe
The universe is constantly chasing after Your love
There is no boundary that could withhold Your love

Space is your definition of ultimate freedom
You carefully imagined a perfect vessel to carry Your love
A flagbearer and ambassador that can represent Your love
to the utmost
Someone like me
I'll spend my whole life
Discovering how much You love me

It's amazing how deep Your love goes
How far Your blood flows
It covered sin and the grave
It washed me white as snow
And made me realize
There's no end to Your love
Your love is eternity

Day 38

Shield of Faith

Above all, taking the shield of faith with which you will be able to quench all the fiery darts of the wicked one. - Ephesians 6:16 NKJV

Your shield of faith protects more than yourself. When Paul was writing about the armor of God, the shield that was widely used was called the, "scutum." It was a large rectangular shield. It was primarily made of wood, a leather covering, and a bit of cloth lining.

The Roman army was a fearsome foe. They deployed their men in groups. They would hold their shields to the left to protect their neighbor. When done correctly, they formed a wall. The men would move in sync with each other; careful not to break formation. They would keep marching forward in this stance: relying on their neighbor to defend them. If one man was taken out, the formation would fall apart and they would have to regroup immediately.

To prevent their shields from catching fire and to maintain the leather they would baptize their shield in water. Arrows of fire and other flaming projectiles would be quenched. Weapon strikes would also slide off.

They had defensive maneuvers and offensive maneuvers. On defense, if they switched to a tortoise stance you can bet no projectile would get through. Men in the middle would hold their shields above their heads to protect from falling projectiles. All the men would bring their shields as close as possible so there would be no space for a weapon to get through. On offense, they would push forward at the same time to break the enemy line and force them out of formation. Once they saw an opening, they would use their spears to pick off the enemies.

Our faith protects more than just ourselves. Our prayers of faith for our families, co-workers, friends, and government are impactful. Our faith to heal others in Jesus' name impacts others. Our faith moves mountains and splits seas to make paths for others to cross. Moses' obedience allowed Israel to cross unharmed; so it is with our faith. You make a way for others.

We have to be refreshed by the Holy Spirit to protect our faith. He encourages us when things happen. He reminds us of His goodness and deliverance. He shows us a good future free of chains and full of hope. It's vitally important that we find our strength in Him! We can do nothing of our self. We certainly try at times but the flesh always fails. Jesus always wins.

Together, we are a strong army in Christ. We can push back the enemy lines, free prisoners, and declare Jesus' victory to all who will believe. Satan trembles at the thought!

You will defend what you love. Love your brothers and sisters in Christ and together make a stand in Christ. We will have an impact on our generation. The fervent prayer of a righteous man or woman avails much! Keep your shield of faith held up and press on!

Night 38

Spectrum of Grace

A full spectrum of grace
Covers the sky
Multicolored streams of light
Wrap the clouds
A magnificent sight
Yet even more beautiful promises
He's inked His will in the clouds
He's painted His Grace across the sky

Red is for Your blood that erased sin
Made us righteous and white as snow

Orange is for Your matchless Glory
For what can compare to Your splendor

Yellow is for Your radiant light
That destroyed darkness and shines in us

Green is for Your abundant provision
There's no good thing that You withhold from us

Blue is for Your far-reaching freedom
For through You our chains have been broken

Indigo is for Your overwhelming forgiveness
Like an ocean it has flooded humanity

Violet is for Your royalty
Lord of Lords and King of Kings You will reign for eternity

When I see the sky filled with such promises
My heart leaps for joy and I praise Your name
Hallelujah, what a loving Savior
For as long as the Earth remains
Your love and Grace shall cover us

Day 39

Sword of God

*For the Word of God is quick, and powerful,
and sharper than any two-edged sword... -
Hebrews 4:12 NKJV*

We are to be quick: ready at a moment's notice. Ready in and out of season. Be available to give a testimony the instant we are called on or led to. We are to be sensitive to the Holy Spirit's voice and guidance.

In Greek, the word used here for quick is "zaō," which is the root word of "zōē". The same word for salvation. It means a variety of things, but what we are focused on is, "active, powerful, efficacious," and "full of vigor." The Word of God is alive and life-giving! It is dynamic and effective. It is full of life. It is the source of all life. Healing, peace, and prosperity are found only in the Word of God!

His Word is powerful. The Greek Word here is "energēs," which translates to effectual. The Lord's Word never returns void or without effect. His Word prospers where it is sent and accomplishes His good will and purpose: always without fail!

His Word is sharp: able to cut with precision. We can know just what and how to say or do something to touch someone's life. God knows what people need. He reveals Himself to others through His children's acts of kindness and love.

Do you find it interesting that the author compares the Word with a two-edged sword? David's Psalms mentioned the term, "sword," to relate to a person's tongue or what they are saying. In addition, "distomos," the Greek word for sword, has an interesting root: "stoma," which translates to mouth. This would mean that the Word of God is stronger than any other words spoken against you!

His spoken Word will make an impact. Confess the Word of God over yourself, your family, your job, your finances, your household, your friends, your country, and you will see change! You will see victory manifest as you speak His Word!

Night 39

Nothing Impossible

You made it
You can change it
All things can be done

Matter bends at Your will
Time is unbound
Atoms mold into anything

Space is stretched
No distance too far
Everything within reach

Speaker of Infinite Possibilities
Doer of Miraculous Feats
Lover of All Mankind

No law You can't break
No matter You can't shape
No dream You can't wake

No mountain too tall
No valley too deep
No ocean too wide

With one Word
A path is made
And Light leads on

Situations get better
Sick become healed
Hearts are pieced together

Transformation occurs
When we receive Your love
Never can we be the same

Old nature is dead
Buried in the grave
Newness of life is ours

Giver of Every Blessing
Provider for Every Need
Abundance Incarnate

Standard of Goodness
Banner of Affection
Shield of Favor

Your glory raises us up
Your mercy rests on us
Your peace watches over us

We can't begin to understand
Just how much You gave for us
A perfect sacrifice, for unclean beings

You traded Your glory
For our shame
And all sin

Eternal joy you wanted to share
Unshakable hope without compare
Passionate and boundless love for all

My heart is Yours
My soul desires You
My life is changed for good

I delight myself in You
I speak Your promises out
I believe every word You've said

You've given me a vision
To accomplish Your mission
Along with all the provision

I trust in You
You'll never let me down
You always lift me up

Off the ground
Above everything
Into Your Heavenly presence

Seated with Christ
My Lord and co-heir
Ruling and reigning over all

Not a care or worry
No issue or trouble
Will shake me off Your lap

I'm with You forever
You're with me forever
We'll always be together

Day 40

Commissioned to Win

15 And He said unto them, "Go ye into all the world, and preach the gospel to every creature. 16 He that believeth and is baptized shall be saved; but he that believeth not shall be damned. 17 And these signs shall follow them that believe; In My name shall they cast out devils; they shall speak with new tongues; 18 They shall take up serpents; and if they drink any deadly thing, it shall not hurt them; they shall lay hands on the sick, and they shall recover." 19 So then after the Lord had spoken unto them, He was received up into heaven, and sat on the right hand of God. - Mark 16:15-19 KJV

GO: we must take the initiative to go. The Lord needs us to be active. We must put our hand to something in order for it to be blessed. We must try different things until we find our calling in the body of Christ.

EVERY CREATURE: we must preach the Word of God to everything around us. We take dominion of the atmosphere around us. Death and Life are in the power of the tongue. Speak life into every dead situation and see it revive. Speak those things that are not as though they are and materialize them in the natural realm.

BAPTIZED: be baptized with Jesus' blood, accept the remission of your sins and receive forgiveness. Let the old man's tendencies be washed away by the blood of Christ through the process of baptism.

FOLLOW THEM: signs accompany the Word of God when He is preached. Expect to see healings and miracles take place where the Word is taught and Jesus glorified!

IN MY NAME: we have been given the privilege to use Jesus' name. In His name there is authority to bind and loose anything that is not good. His name is above every other name!

CAST OUT DEVILS: demons cannot resist the authority of Jesus' name. They must go and leave at the sound of His name. He is above them and they tremble when He is welcomed into the situation.

SPEAK IN NEW TONGUES: foreshadow of the Holy Spirit's baptism. Surrendering the tongue can only be done through God. The tongue can only be subdued when given over to God.

TAKE UP SERPENTS: we're able to recognize when the Word of God is being twisted to fit opinions of men. The serpents are sly doctrine. They are carefully hidden: ready to ambush. We are able to realize what is Truth when we have been baptized into the Holy Spirit who leads us into all Truth, understanding and knowledge.

DRINK ANY DEADLY THING: the attacks of the enemy will not affect us! The only way you would drink a deadly thing is if you are being tricked by an enemy or they slipped something into your drink. We will come out stronger as we shake off his attempts at taking us out.

LAY HANDS ON THE SICK: laying hands is symbolic of exerting authority. Speaking Jesus' name and taking authority over the sickness will force it to leave. Hands provide a channel for the river of the Life of Christ to flow through.

SAT ON THE RIGHT HAND: place of authority, at the King's side, rested and at peace. The work is finished, complete, and now He is basking in victory forevermore. He has invited us to sit with Him in victory!

Night 40

Warrior of Love

Imprisoned in darkness and shame
Held ransom by sin's claim
An army of one
Shouted through the walls

With a voice like a trumpet
He told me, "Do not fear!"
I turned to see
A Man who gave His all for me

My hope was rising
Yet I was not convinced
I'd been here as long as I could remember
I could see no end

He stormed the gates
And laid waste to the pain
That was binding me up
And holding me down

He said, "I'm coming for you!
I was sent by Love
To bring you home.
No matter the cost."

I heard His voice
Getting closer and closer
As He was cutting a path
Through my enemies

Bursting through
The prison door
With a joyful smile
He ripped open my cage

He held out His hand
And said, "Come.
Let's go home to
Where you belong."

Surprised and amazed
I met hope that day
I was too weak to reach out
Even though I really tried

He picked me up
And carried me
Out of the dark
Into His light

I looked around
And all I saw
Was total destruction
Not one soldier stood tall

He was so happy
That He finally found me
He said, "Let's throw a party
When we get home!"

Who is this Man?
Who knows my name?
I thought I was alone
And that no one cared

Yet in His arms
I felt a peace
I couldn't explain
I never want to leave

I asked Him His name
And He said,
"My name is Jesus,
Warrior of Love."

"I was sent by My Father.
To rescue you
And reunite you
With your true family."

"Why would You do this?
What am I to You?
I can't be worth
All this trouble."

With a hearty chuckle
He said, "I love you.
No other reason
is needed."

"I'd never felt
A love like this.
But I believe
I can trust You."

He said, "Don't worry
I'll never leave you.
You can count on Me.
I'll always be with you."

In an instant
We made it to His kingdom
At the gate
He said, "His child has come home."

I could not count
All the people
Who celebrated with us
As we walked in

He took me to see
The King of this land
Nervous and frightened
I did not know what to think

Jesus said, "The King
Has been waiting
For my return.
Surely, He wants to see your face."

I walked to the throne room
Jesus with me
Before I can make it
To the end of the aisle

The King jumps off of His throne
And ran towards me
He embraced me
And said, "Welcome home, My child."

Overwhelmed with
Emotion and belonging
I said "Yes,
I am home."

He had been waiting
For this moment
"Now come with Me.
I have gifts for you."

He gave me a royal
Robe of righteousness
He gave me a ring
With His name on it

He gave me His Word
To study and learn
He gave me Holy Spirit
To lead and guide

And Jesus
Warrior of Love
Will always be
By my side

I still remember
What it felt like
To have no hope
No future in sight

But now with Jesus
I know what it's like
To have a real family
Who holds me tight

No demon
No angel
No person
Can separate Him from me

Forever and ever
I'll cling
To Jesus
Warrior of Love

Review Days 31-40

Sending in Power

Sharing of your wine: joyfully starting parties wherever you go

You have been actualized. Your faith is stronger. Your relationship with God is deeper. Your gifts and callings are seen in operation. You flow in the Holy Spirit. You are equipped to speak and demonstrate the Word of God to any who come along your path. You know who you are in Christ. You are available to partner with God to bring Heaven to Earth as a spring of blessing and refreshing love to those around you. Go forth. Share the Gospel with every creature. You are ready and willing to pursue the Great Commission in compassionate love for your brethren and soon-to-be brothers and sisters. Here's a prayer to send you in power.

"Lord, I thank You for making me into a blessing. You have given me so much to share and to give to others. Jesus, help me to see the opportunities around me. I speak in boldness the things of God. I see the sick getting healed. I see people learning their true identity in You. I see miracles happening before my eyes. I see the dead coming back to life. It's all because of You, Jesus. You work mightily through me to bring Heaven to Earth. I am a powerful conqueror in Jesus' name. Satan trembles when I wake up each morning. I shall set the captives free and break every chain of bondage in Jesus' name. Satan can do nothing but watch in fear as I tear down His strongholds of evil. Thank You Lord, I am thankful for the love, goodness, peace, joy, and wisdom you give me. Surround me with Your angelic messengers to prepare the soil of the hearts of Your people in advance, so they will be quick to receive Your Word as incorruptible seed. Now, I go forth in the power of Your might to take back Your children from Satan. All for the glory of God. In Jesus' precious name I pray, Amen."

Concluding Exhortation

BY PAMELA LYNN

This is one of the most breathtaking devotions I have ever read! It is also very unique in its nature whereby the author is divinely inspired by the Holy Spirit to give His teachings in the morning to ponder on during the day, and beautiful poems to be read before bedtime for a sweet and peaceful sleep!

I met Aaron at Charis Bible College Indianapolis in 2017 at a hybrid school in Fishers, IN. I started out knowing he liked writing and singing songs, even though I hadn't heard any of them until the Spring of 2020. He asked me to join in with him and others on his online, 'Praise Without Ceasing,' ministry. His love for the Lord pours out when he plays and sings! It's a wonderful time for all to sing-along with him and praise the Lord! As an open vessel for the Lord, Aaron has a way of pouring out those blessings on to others around him!

But, Aaron hasn't always liked to write. Aaron has confided in me that when he was younger he didn't much like writing. So that was definitely a confirmation to me that, "all," his writings are inspired by the Holy Spirit. Another confirmation is that anytime I read something that Aaron has written, I am so moved and blessed by the Holy Spirit, I believe that he wrote it just for me! A little grandiose sounding I know, but I believe this book will speak to you as well!

To go to Heaven one must be born again. To get the full benefits of this book, you must be filled with the Holy Spirit. If you aren't, just ask God and He will freely give!

So, if you need to re-read this, go ahead. For I did, and I watched the blessings flow, and yes, the next morning I would wake in the sweet presence of the poem I read the night before!

Be Blessed!

Concluding Prayer

BY AUNT BONNIE

We thank You Lord! We praise You for Your Living Word today. As Your Word goes forth in life-changing flow here on Earth from Aaron into us: we believe and perceive that this Word will not return unto You, Lord, void, but will accomplish all the purpose you have planned for us! Jesus, You love us and we love You! Thank You, for providing for our every need and even the ones we didn't know we had.

We're marching upward to Zion to meet You at Your coming. As your Living Word richly dwells in us and our vessels and wineskins are made new; we are made finer and refined and are becoming perfect and finished works of Your Saving Grace. Thank You, for pouring out the finest vintage of Your love into us. Thank You Lord, for these 40 days of aging the vintage to perfection for all the ages to come!

Now Lord, we enjoy, take heed, and receive of Your Holy Spirit. We are exceedingly and abundantly blessed beyond all measure from You, Jesus, and Your Holy Spirit. Thank You, for seeking us and desiring to repair, rebuild, and restore us unto You. Help us to bring all Your children into the Kingdom of God to be made completely new through You for Your Glory! Hallelujah! Thank You Lord!

In Jesus' name, Amen!

Making of the Book

Thank you, for supporting me. This was my first book. I had no intention of writing it. One day, I was scrolling through my notes on my phone and saw I had a bunch of them. A random thought (actually Holy Spirit) came to my mind that I have enough here for a book. I quickly dismissed it. I had no time to write a book along with all my other responsibilities. I kept trying to tell myself, "I don't have time for that, Lord." The Lord had enough and said to me, "You've already got it in these notes. Start organizing. There are several books here." Again I was like, "Fine, but I thought the novel was going to be my first book?" He said, "Nope, I need you to work on a different book. Start reading your notes, you'll see what I'm getting at." I was still quite puzzled but as a good child of God, I put it off for days. He had to remind me, "Are you going to organize your notes?" I told Him, "Yeah, I'll do it now." I began to look at my notes and found many teachings that were short, concise, and shareable. I wondered if I could make a devotional out of them. "Is this the book you wanted me to make?" No answer, but I did get a peaceful feeling about it.

I started a spreadsheet and began putting the teachings and poetry into it. "How many days is this supposed to be?" He said, "40 Days." I was not sure how I would do 40 days worth. However, I continued going through my teachings and Facebook Posts. I got up to a hefty number. The hard part, was choosing what to put into the book. It took several weeks of determining what material to put into it. I switched things around frequently. I played around with the numbering. It was W O R K. However, I began to think about 40 days and nights. Noah's ark came to mind. It rained for 40 days and nights. For some reason, nights stuck out to me. Shouldn't I have something happen at night too? I pondered that for days.

I had more than enough material for 40 days but something seemed off. I have all these poems the Lord gave me but was not finding a good way to implement them into the devotion. Then, it hit me, why don't I read a poem at the end of the night? That would be the night part of each day. I started getting excited and broke the spreadsheet into days and nights. I separated both out and found I needed more poems. I was inspired by Holy Spirit to write a lot around this time. The poems flowed so naturally. It was as if the book was writing itself.

2 weeks later, I was ready to start arranging it as a book. I started a Google Document and began to lay out the days and nights in sequential order. It was a long and arduous process. Once I got it to a reasonable format, I shared it with Pam. She was so excited to read it. She read it, gave me honest feedback, and enjoyed the premise. I didn't give her the 40 days to look it over though. I was in a hurry to make it happen. I mentioned the book to my Aunt Bonnie and she said she'd love to read it. I emailed it to her. She printed it out and began to read it and give me feedback. She said she loved it. That she needed it. It was exactly what the Lord needed to give her. She gave me much feedback, and from that point on, was heavily involved in

the book making process. I also sent the book to my good friend Pastor Jay. He looked it over, edited it professionally, and was happy to read it. After getting such positive feedback, I decided to pursue harder.

After about 6 weeks the next revision saw the addition of verses for each day, study verses for each day, 10 day sections, prayer of salvation, prayer for Baptism of Holy Spirit, an intro & bio, foreword, concluding exhortation, and concluding prayer. It took me and Aunt Bonnie much time to sift through the days and nights and better match the days and nights together while also putting them in a logical order. After we got that much done, we were ready to begin the next read through. This time, we were going to take the full 40 days and run through it as intended. I met a great friend through Crossroads School of Chaplaincy. I mentioned my book and Paula said she'd love to read it when it is published. I decided to include her in the book reading group. We all started on the 1st of January of 2021.

After the 40 days were up I was excited to make more changes. I got feedback from my readers and made some more decisions. I moved all the scriptures on each day and night to a Related Scriptures section. I added the Special Thanks section, I added 10 day section reviews, and made many edits to the content throughout the book.

And that is where we are today. I wanted strongly to publish on or near my birthday of March 4th. Why? March 4th (forth) is such a prophetic day. This book helps the Body of Christ march forth into victory and power to proclaim the Gospel of Jesus to the world with signs following. So with that being said, I thank you again for your support. I believe many more books are still to come in Jesus' name for His glory!

With all of Love's blessings,
Aaron Beach

Related Scriptures

Day 1 - Variety is the Spice of Life: Guidance - Psalms 119:105; God's Plan - Jeremiah 29:11; Blessing - Deuteronomy 28:8
Night 1 - Look: Creation - John 1:1; Stars and Sand - Genesis 22:17; Hope - Psalms 78:7

Day 2 - Life is Attracted to Life: Path - Psalms 16:11; Truth - John 8:32; Life - 1 John 4:9
Night 2 - Enough: Provider - Isaiah 58:11; Faithfulness - 2 Timothy 2:13; Value - Luke 12:7

Day 3 - Receive His Love: Love - 1 John 4:10; Love - Romans 5:8; Gifts - James 1:17
Night 3 - Live to Love: Love - 1 John 4:7; Work of Ministry - 1 Peter 4:11; Jesus' Ministry - Luke 4:18

Day 4 - East and West: Dead to Sin - Romans 6:11; New Nature - Ephesians 4:24; Righteousness - 2 Corinthians 5:21
Night 4 - Finally I'm Free: He Hears Us - Psalms 40:1; Redeemer - Isaiah 47:4; Grace and Truth - John 1:14

Day 5 - Walk in Peace: Direct - Proverbs 16:9; Path - Jeremiah 10:23; Straight - Hebrews 12:13
Night 5 - Not Alone: Never Forsake - Hebrews 13:5; Leads Us - Isaiah 42:16; Father - Galatians 4:6

Day 6 - Flow in the Current: Blood - Ephesians 1:7; River of Life - Ezekiel 47:9; Stability - Hebrews 13:8

Night 6 - Waterfall of Love: Water - Isaiah 41:18; River - Psalms 36:8; Well - John 4:14

Day 7 - Like Your Father: Father - Proverbs 4:1; Paths of Righteousness - Psalms 23:3; In His Image - Genesis 1:26
Night 7 - Someone: Comforter - John 14:18; Stone Heart - Ezekiel 11:19; Easy Yoke - Matthew 11:28

Day 8 - Body Heat: Shadow - Colossians 2:17; Light - Daniel 2:22; Holy Spirit - Romans 15:13
Night 8 - Flawless: Jesus - Revelation 19:12; Lamb of God - John 1:29; Joy - 1 Peter 1:8

Day 9 - Appreciate God: Pearl - Matthew 13:46; Thanks - Psalms 140:13; Thanks - Colossians 3:17
Night 9 - Everything to Me: Created - Psalms 139:14; God's Joy - Zephaniah 3:17; Safety - Psalms 32:7

Day 10 - The Ultimate Program: Healing - Psalms 103:3; Provision - 2 Corinthians 9:8; Peace - Isaiah 9:6
Night 10 - Have and to Hold: Potter - Isaiah 64:8; Savior - Psalms 34:18; Protection - Psalms 91:7

Review Days 1-10 - Salvation: New Heart - Ezekiel 36:26; New Creation - 2 Corinthians 5:17; Confess & Believe - Romans 10:9-13; Made Righteous - 2 Corinthians 5:21; Believe in Jesus - Acts 16:31

Day 11 - Taste and See: Bread of Life - John 6:35; Meditate - Joshua 1:8; Spring - Isaiah 58:11
Night 11 - Come to My Table: Table - Psalms 23:5; Love and Peace - 2 Corinthians 13:11; Comfort - Psalms 71:21

Day 12 - Feed on Jesus: Yoke - Matthew 11:30; Water of Life - Revelation 21:6; Thinking - Proverbs 23:7

Night 12 - Thanks to Your Love: Armor - Ephesians 6:13; Completion - Philippian 1:6; Conqueror - Romans 8:37

Day 13 - Spring Restored: Well - Isaiah 12:3; Spirit - Romans 8:11; Life - 2 Timothy 1:10
Night 13 - Open Vessel: Rain - 1 King 18:41; Love - 1 Peter 1:22; Children - Galatians 3:26

Day 14 - Receive from the Table: Grace - Romans 5:20; Communion - 1 Corinthians 11:26; Finished - Isaiah 53:11
Night 14 - Run to Your Table: Dwell - Psalms 84:4; Throne Room - Hebrews 4:16; Justification - Galatians 3:11

Day 15 - Sun of Righteousness: Light - John 12:46; Sun - Psalms 84:11; Meditate - Psalms 1:2
Night 15 - Universe of Love: Creation - Hebrews 1:2; Light - Isaiah 58:10; Joy - Psalms 89:15

Day 16 - Starlight: Fear of the Lord - Isaiah 33:6; Renewed Mind - Ephesians 4:23; Treasure - Luke 12:34
Night 16 - Cosmic Painter: Sun and Moon - Genesis 1:16; Stars - Psalms 147:4; Stars - Jeremiah 31:35

Day 17 - Trust Him: God's Way - 2 Samuel 22:33; Strength - Psalms 18:32; God Will Help - Isaiah 50:7
Night 17 - Dream: Salvation - Joel 2:32; Desire - Psalms 145:19; Faithfulness - Hebrews 10:23

Day 18 - Automatic Updates: Daily - Lamentations 3:22-23; Correction - Proverbs 13:18; Renewal - 2 Corinthians 4:16
Night 18 - Not a Wretch: Freedom - Romans 6:22; Image - 2 Corinthians 3:18; Name - Isaiah 56:5

Day 19 - Believe God: Strongholds - 2 Corinthians 10:4; Heart - Isaiah 29:13; Hope - Proverbs 15:30
Night 19 - He's Got This: Evil - John 17:15; Hope - Psalms 42:5; Good Instead of Evil - Genesis 50:20

Day 20 - Christ is Your Faith: Faith and Love - Romans 12:3; Jesus - Luke 2:52; Faith - 2 Timothy 1:13
Night 20 - Why?: Holy Spirit - 1 Corinthians 3:16; Spirit - Zechariah 4:6; Power - 1 Thessalonians 1:5

Review Days 11-20 - Baptism of the Holy Spirit: Speak in New Languages - Mark 16:17; Promised Holy Spirit - Luke 24:49; Receive Power - Acts 1:8; Control Your Tongue - James 3:2; Ask, Seek, and Knock - Luke 11:10, 13; Comforter - John 14:16; Pentecost and Holy Spirit - Acts 2:1-4

Day 21 - Take Him Out of the Box: Possible - Matthew 19:26; Faith - 1 Corinthians 16:13; Limits - Psalms 71:15
Night 21 - Letter to My Bride: Good - Psalms 34:10; Comforter - John 14:26; Bride - Isaiah 61:10

Day 22 - God Wants You Free: Freedom - 2 Corinthians 3:17; Free from Religion - Galatians 5:1; Dwelling - Ephesians 2:22
Night 22 - Army of Christ: Body of Christ - 1 Corinthians 12:12; Sword - Ephesians 6:17; Dominion - Genesis 1:28

Day 23 - Created in Joy: Joy - Psalms 21:1; Joy - Habakkuk 3:18; Joy - Colossians 1:11
Night 23 - Bubble: Brevity of Life - Psalms 144:3; Light - Revelation 22:5; Deliverance - Proverbs 11:8

Day 24 - No More Thorns: Thorns - Genesis 3:18; Blessing - Galatians 3:13; Heirs - Ephesians 3:6

Night 24 - Lord of the Seasons: Blessing - Isaiah 30:23; Rain - Ezekiel 34:26; Blessing - Deuteronomy 28:12

Day 25 - Guard Your Tongue: Power of Tongue - Proverbs 18:21; Tongue - James 3:10; Withheld Tongue - Luke 1:20
Night 25 - Anthem of Praise: Praise - Psalms 52:9; Singing - Zephaniah 3:14; Worthy - Revelation 5:12

Day 26 - Will of Jesus: Heirs - Titus 3:7; Heirs of the Promise - Romans 9:8; In His Will - 1 John 5:14
Night 26 - El Shaddai: El Shaddai - Genesis 17:1; Birds - Matthew 6:26; Supply - Philippians 4:19

Day 27 - Kingdom of God: Kings and Priests - Revelation 5:10; Heirs - James 2:5; Kingdom - 1 Peter 2:9
Night 27 - Answer: Wake Up - Proverbs 6:9; Action - Acts 3:6; What God Wants - James 1:27

Day 28 - Demand the Promise: Ask - Matthew 7:8; Inheritance - Colossians 1:12; Finished - John 17:4
Night 28 - Thrive: Live - Psalms 118:17; Rest - Hebrews 4:10; Grace - 1 Timothy 1:14

Day 29 - Why Are You Waiting?: Now - Hebrews 11:1; Salvation - 1 Chronicles 16:23; Salvation - Isaiah 25:9
Night 29 - Waiting: Patience - James 1:3; Rest - 1 Peter 1:13; Victory - 2 Corinthians 2:14

Day 30 - Victory is Yours: Victory - 1 Corinthians 15:57; Promise - Hebrews 8:6; Declare - Daniel 4:2
Night 30 - I AM: I AM - Exodus 3:14; Accepted - Ephesians 1:6; Equipped - Hebrews 13:21

Review Days 21-30 - Consecration: Consecration of Priests - Exodus 29; Commissioning of Paul and Barnabas - Acts 13:2; Clean Heart - Psalms 51:10

Day 31 - Faith Produces an Action: Faith and Action - James 2:26; Hope - 2 Timothy 2:16; Word - Deuteronomy 30:14

Night 31 - I Thank You: Thanks - 1 Thessalonians 5:18; Honor - Revelation 5:13; Sacrifice of Praise - Hebrews 13:15

Day 32 - We Cannot Be Separated: Power - Isaiah 55:11; Healing - Acts 10:38; Faith - Luke 17:6

Night 32 - I Am Supernatural: New Creation - 2 Corinthians 5:17; Healing - Isaiah 53:4-5; Faith - Galatians 2:20

Day 33 - Downloading from God: Asking - Philippians 4:6-7; Faith - Hebrews 11:6; Patience - 1 Thessalonians 1:2-4

Night 33 - I'll Never Find Out: Hope - Romans 5:5; Calm - Psalms 107:28; Taught - Proverbs 4:4

Day 34 - Jesus' Fire: Witness - Luke 24:49; Fire - Isaiah 10:17; Power - Daniel 3:27

Night 34 - Paid the Price: Pearl - Match 13:46; Save the World - John 3:16-17; Reconciliation - 2 Corinthians 5:18

Day 35 - Rely on Your Shepherd: Shepherd - 1 Peter 2:25; Hear - Psalms 85:8; Obey - Hebrews 3:18

Night 35 - Tarry: Presence - Psalms 16:11; Instruction - Job 22:22; Relationship - Jeremiah 15:16

Day 36 - Answer the Phone: Words - Jeremiah 1:9; Holy Spirit - 1 Corinthians 12:4-11; Love - 1 Peter 1:22

Night 36 - I Delight in You: Chosen - Ephesians 1:4; Walk - 1 Thessalonians 2:12; Children of God - 1 John 3:2

Day 37 - Love is a Plus: Compassion - Matthews 9:35-38; Jesus Revealed - Hebrews 1:1-2; Evangelism - 1 Corinthians 9:22

Night 37 - Love is Eternity: Universe - Psalms 33:6; Redemption of Sin - Hebrews 9:28; Everlasting Love - Jeremiah 31:3

Day 38 - Shield of Faith: Shield - 2 Samuel 22:33-38; Love - 1 John 3:11; Unity - Ephesians 4:13

Night 38 - Spectrum of Grace: Rainbow - Genesis 9:16; White as Snow - Isaiah 1:18; Forgiveness - Micah 7:19

Day 39 - Sword of God: Ready - 2 Timothy 4:2; Praise - Psalms 149:6; Declare - Job 22:28

Night 39 - Nothing is Impossible: Possibility - Genesis 18:14; Path - Psalms 119:35; Above - Colossians 3:1

Day 40 - Commissioned to Win: Matthew 10:1; Great Commission - Luke 9:1-2; Ministry - Isaiah 61:1-3

Night 40 - Warrior of Love: Isaiah 61:7; Prison - Psalms 107:14; Restoration - Jeremiah 33:6-9

Review Days 31-40 - Sending: Faith Works by Love - Galatians 5:6; Word Confirmed with Signs - Mark 16:15-20; Who Can Stand Against Us - Romans 8:31-39

Get in Touch

I would love to hear what you have to say! If you have a testimony, a prayer request, or just want to say hi, you can visit my website at *https://PraiseWithoutCeasing.online* or email me at *info@PraiseWithoutCeasing.online*. If you would like to support my ministry you can give with PayPal or CashApp. **Thank you for your support!**

Scan & go to my
website

Cashapp -
$narotosensei

Paypal.me/aarbea